DR. BECKY BARABE

The Only Educators' Grant Writing Guide You Will Ever Need

Developing A Successful Proposal With Proven Strategies That Get Funded

Copyright © 2024 by Dr. Becky Barabe

All rights reserved. No part of this publication may be reproduced, stored or transmitted in any form or by any means, electronic, mechanical, photocopying, recording, scanning, or otherwise without written permission from the publisher. It is illegal to copy this book, post it to a website, or distribute it by any other means without permission.

Dr. Becky Barabe asserts the moral right to be identified as the author of this work.

Dr. Becky Barabe has no responsibility for the persistence or accuracy of URLs for external or third-party Internet Websites referred to in this publication and does not guarantee that any content on such Websites is, or will remain, accurate or appropriate.

Designations used by companies to distinguish their products are often claimed as trademarks. All brand names and product names used in this book and on its cover are trade names, service marks, trademarks and registered trademarks of their respective owners. The publishers and the book are not associated with any product or vendor mentioned in this book. None of the companies referenced within the book have endorsed the book.

First edition

This book was professionally typeset on Reedsy.
Find out more at reedsy.com

Contents

Introduction	1
Chapter 1	3
Chapter 2	12
Chapter 3	14
Chapter 4	15
Chapter 5	17
Chapter 6	19
Chapter 7	21
Chapter 8	23
Chapter 9	28
Chapter 10	32
Conclusion	35

Introduction

Welcome to the Only Educators' Grant Writing Guide You Will Ever Need: Developing A Successful Proposal with Proven Strategies That Get Funded. My name is Becky Barabé, and I am extremely excited to be writing this guide for you! I am thrilled to have this perfect quick start to give to colleagues when they ask about how to get started in grants, rather than needing to give them a whole presentation or sit down discussion about all the things they need to do to write a successful grant proposal.

The other reason I am so excited to be writing this guide is that the world of grants has given me so much joy, providing an opportunity to dream big and then see projects come to fruition in the real world. It has also allowed me to foster partnerships across various sectors to support individual, community, or regional economic and community development for the betterment of the populations I have served over the years.

A brief background about myself…I have been writing and receiving grants as well as managing grant-funded projects for over 25 years now. I started as a recent college graduate supporting a group of high school and community college educators with a planning grant, that then turned into the chance to write for the implementation grant, and once awarded I was lucky enough to be hired into the project manager role. That was the start of my career with grants, and I was hooked!

Now after years of experience in the grants business, I can proudly say that I have worked for K-12 school districts, county offices of education, community colleges, and public and private universities in partnership with non-profits, public agencies, city and country departments, businesses and industry, and various associations or community groups. I have established many educational partnerships and implemented hundreds of projects and programs. With over $500 million dollars in grant awards and seeing the organization, population served, and community or region change for the better, I know firsthand that grants can and do have a huge impact on the economic vitality in a geographic area.

This book doesn't need to be read cover to cover. Rather, it is designed in clear components of the grant making process to assist you with each step in the process, or to allow you to jump into the stage you currently find yourself in now.

Now if you are still sitting there getting ready to start your grant, or you have initiated the process and are looking for a little assistance, I am ready to share my experience with you.

With this brief introduction, I am ready to get started. Jump in and join me, today is the day!

Chapter 1

Getting Started

When getting started with grants, there are a few things to keep in mind. One, there is a typical flow to each grant (some variations, but the components tend to be the same core items). Two, there is some data, partnerships, and document collection that will assist you with some of the details as you get started with your framework or idea concepts. Third, have fun! Often you can dream big and then fine tune to the funding source's expectations or parameters as needed. Only you can limit the depth and breadth of your organization's success in grants, so go for it!

Grant Flow

The flow of a grant typically has the following components:

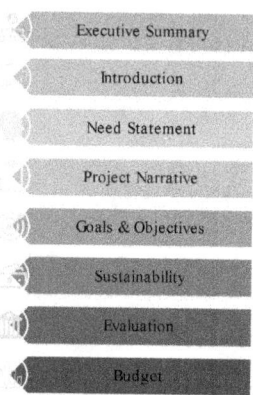

Executive Summary: A short who, what, when, where, and why for the grant as well as costs.

Introduction: Brief overview of who the organization is and how the project objectives and outcomes of the funding source fit with the mission or vision of the organization.

Need Statement: Describes the needs of a population of people in a geographic area.

Project Narrative: Describes the plan and activities that this project will use to address the needs of the target population.

Goals & Objectives: Lays out the details of how the organization will accomplish the project's plan and activities with S.M.A.R.T. goals and objectives to assist with accomplishing the intended outcomes.

Sustainability: Describes the foundation the grant has laid for the organization and how integration into the organization for the long-term can be accomplished once the funding has come to an end.

Evaluation: Provides the details of how the organization will determine if they have been successful in their goals and objectives, or how they will work to improve moving forward.

Budget: Links the funding requested to the activities, goals, and objectives to accomplish the project (personnel, supplies, equipment, etc.).

Data

The data needed for grant applications can come from internal or external resources. Some examples include:

Internal:

- Organizational database
- Past participant feedback or surveys
- Statistics that the organization keeps for other purposes in the process of doing business

External:

- United States Census Bureau: https://www.census.gov/quickfacts/
- State Resources (examples for Education in California):
- K-12 School District: https://www.cde.ca.gov/ds/ad/dataquest.asp

- Community Colleges: https://datamart.cccco.edu/
- Public Universities: https://www.calstate.edu/data-center or https://www.universityofcalifornia.edu/about-us/information-center

Partnerships

Partnerships come in all shapes and sizes, but the basic principle is more than one organization coming together with a likeminded goal. This could include:

Other Educational Organizations:

- K-12 School Districts
- Charter Schools
- Community Colleges
- Public 4-Year Universities
- Private 4-Year Universities
- County Offices of Education
- Parent Education Groups
- K-14 or K-16 Educational Associations/Partnerships
- Early Childhood Education Centers
- After School Programs
- Other Grant Funded Programs

Public Departments or Agencies:

- City Departments or Agencies
- County Departments or Agencies

CHAPTER 1

- State Departments or Agencies
- National Departments or Agencies

Think Education, Employment, Health, Housing, Justice, Transportation, etc.

Workforce & Economic Development Groups:

- Regional Workforce Development Boards
- Economic Development Corporations
- Chambers of Commerce
- Industry Associations
- Businesses

Non-Profit Organizations:

- Local Charity Groups *(think Red Cross, Salvation Army, etc.)*
- Social or Humanitarian Associations *(think Rotary, Kiwanis, etc.)*
- Charitable Organizations
- Private Foundations
- Faith Based Organizations

Organizational Documents

For the organization that will be the grant proposal submitter and lead once funded, it is important to gather some key documents that may be needed throughout the grant process:

Entity Documents:

- Employer Identification Number (EIN)
- Taxpayer Identification Number (TIN)
- Entity Documentation (Non-Profit 501(c)3, LLC, S-Corp, C-Corp, etc.)

Organizational Documents:

- Mission or Vision Statement
- Organizational Chart
- Key Leadership:
- Contact Information
- Resumes
- Job Descriptions
- Brochures or Flyers or Webpages *(think Description of Segments, Departments, or Areas of the Organization)*

Tax Documents:

- Latest Annual Entity Filing
- Latest Tax Returns or Audit Report

Let's Have Fun!

Now that you have thought through and gathered all the tools you need to get started, let the games begin. Now is the time to take the Request for Proposal (RFP) from the funder and get into the brainstorming mode. Most often the funder will outline what they would like you to answer, so you can start with transferring that information out of the RFP and into a Word document outline format.

CHAPTER 1

Then if this is the first time the organization is going after a grant, gather a few folks together to have a kick off meeting and brainstorm ideas, or have some focus group sessions around each of the Grant Flow components mentioned previously. If this is not the first time the organization is working on a grant, ask to have a copy of previous work and whether the project was awarded (if not, ask if feedback from the funder was received in order to provide an improved upon proposal).

Kick Off Meeting or Focus Groups

It is always a good idea to have a kickoff meeting with the leadership or key personnel that will be involved with the grant development and implementation once awarded. This allows for review of the Grant Flow components and to begin gathering any documentation or internal data needed for the proposal.

If the organization is new to grants, I would recommend a few focus groups to get to the bottom of what needs there are for the target population(s) as well as activities that would be helpful to serve the intended populations(s). Also, conversations with key personnel from a programming and data as well as fiscal perspective will allow you to develop the budget, evaluation, and sustainability sections more efficiently.

Once these meetings have taken place it is time to take your notes and start applying them to the grant outline in earnest. When initiating the writing, start each section with a restating of the prompt, such as:

Prompt: Describe the problem to be addressed for this target population.

Sample Sentence for Middle School Population: The problem to be addressed is low Math scores on tests for middle school students for

Fresno County.

Once you have your introductory sentence going, think about 3 supporting sentences and a concluding statement for each section. Or present a bit of detail and support with research, data, or the process you will follow to accomplish the prompt. Each section doesn't need to be lengthy but does need to answer the question asked.

TIP: I will often take the total length of pages that the RFP indicates and then divide that out by the points granted for each section.

For example, based on a grant with 100-point value for the narrative and the request of a maximum of 10 pages in length, double spaced, with 1" margins then I would do the math just to the right. Once I have the number of pages divided by number of total points, I can determine how long each section should be based on page length. This will give you the proper amount of text and information depth that should be the focus of each section. It also shows you where your most meaty parts of the proposal should be and what the funder is most interested in learning about from your organization; in this example the goals and objectives is the meatiest, followed by the Need Statement and Project Narrative.

SECTION	POINTS	PAGES
Executive Summary	1	0.8
Introduction	1	0.8
Need Statement	2	1.6
Project Narrative	2	1.6
Goals & Objectives	3	2.5
Sustainability	1	0.8
Evaluation	1	0.8
Budget	1	0.8

Also, coming up with a catchy project title is an area where you or the organization can highlight your creativity for the project, and is a key piece to naming and establishing a brand for the project. You can use an acronym that can be shortened for your narrative but gives more detail regarding your overall project on the title page or header. Or just an aspirational catch phrase that summarizes the intent of your project and can be used in marketing the project once funded.

Chapter 2

Executive Summary

Now remember, an Executive Summary is a short who, what, when, where, and why for the grant as well as costs in typically one page of narrative. While this section is at the start of the grant application package, it is often written after the rest of the narrative is completed, to be in sync with the grant narrative details but can be written as an overview in the beginning to give the organization some focus points to consider as a project proposal. Each of these key targets will only be 1-2 paragraphs.

In the Executive Summary start by sharing with the funder "who" the organization is that is writing this grant (more details can be found in the grant narrative's Introduction section).Then explain the high-level points of "what" the funding will be used for and the expected timeline of "when"; typically, this is done in bullet format to emphasize the objectives of the grant (more details will be provided in the Project Narrative as well as Goals and Objectives sections). The "where" provides a few key data points that point toward the dire need for the funding as it relates to the geographic area or target population

CHAPTER 2

(more details will be given in the Need Statement section). The "why" is the part of the Executive Summary that explains why getting this funding would provide such an impact for the target population to be served (more details will be linked in the Sustainability Plan and Evaluation Plan sections). This of these 5 points as the reason why the funder should provide the funding being asked for. With the conclusion of the "cost", there should be a 1-page pitch to the funder of the overall project concept and the amount of funding being requested for their consideration (more details are in the Budget and Budget Narrative sections).

Chapter 3

Introduction

The Introduction is a brief overview of who the organization is and how the project objectives and outcomes of the funding source fit with the mission or vision of the organization. Think of this narrative as the link between the organization you are writing the grant application for, and the funding source; providing a clear connection to the purpose and activities that the funding source would like to support.

In the Introduction start by sharing with the funder the organization's background, including when it was established or how many years it has been in operation. Provide a little bit of details on the type of entity it is and how its structure is set up. Also, explain the target population(s) the organization serves and how the organization is poised to utilize the grant funds to expand its reach or scope to provide additional services. If possible, provide a clear connection with the mission or vision of the organization and the funding source.

Chapter 4

Need Statement

The Need Statement describes the needs of a population of people in a geographic area. This will often include data that paints a picture of the dire need of the community or individuals that will be served (this is what you want to show to be able to flip the narrative in the Project Narrative and Goals and Objectives sections, indicating that with this grant funding these negative aspects can be mitigated to some extent). The data will typically come for local city or county statistics as well as state or national statistics.

In the Need Statement start by presenting key statics that are relevant to the grant. The more you can drill down the data to the population being served the better. If the target population being served is sub-par to the state or national averages, highlight that for the grant reader. This section brings up the *pain points* such as poverty, lack of educational attainment, housing insecurities, high levels of teen pregnancies, or health disparities to name a few examples.When writing the Need Statement, you don't call these items mentioned *pain points*, but you do want to show the status of the target population and why grant funding is needed to combat these issue areas. Much of this information may be put into informational charts accompanied by a sentence or two explaining the data in the chart or highlighting the target population's status in comparison to the local, state, or national averages.

TIP: Think of this section as what are the "pain points" or the "woe is me/us" portion of the grant. If everything was perfectly great, there would be no reason for the funder to fund the organization. So, the funder that their funding is needed.

Chapter 5

Project Narrative

The Project Narrative describes the plan and steps that this project will use to address the needs of the target population. This is typically the meatiest portion of the grant application, with explanations of how the grant funding will serve the target population as well as what the organization hopes to accomplish with the funds. Oftentimes, the Request for Proposal (RFP) will outline some of the key activities the funder would like to see in the narrative; follow these prompts if made available, or if there is a list of suggestions try to incorporate as many as are feasible for the organization.

In the Project Narrative you will be presenting the activities the organization intends to provide with the grant funds. Each activity should have its own paragraph (or more) explaining the purpose and intended outcomes or support that will be provided. This section then dovetails with the Goals and Objectives section below.

TIP: Think of this section as what solutions to the "pain points" mentioned in the Need Statement. Tell the funder how the organization intends to combat the negativity in the target population(s) with activities that will improve the outcomes and change lives. This is the "pitch" for why the organization should receive funds, and it must be compelling and well thought through.

Chapter 6

Goals and Objectives

The Goals and Objectives detail how the organization will accomplish the project's plan with S.M.A.R.T. goals to assist with accomplishing the intended tasks. This is typically represented in chart format and provides a specific goal that is measurable, achievable, realistic, and has an associated timeframe. Often it will be coupled with people responsible for the goal and sometimes a link to the financial cost associated with each goal.

In the Goals and Objectives section, you are often restating the activities from the Project Narrative, but in this chart-type format. The activities should blend into the goals and objectives and will often form a Work Plan that has a goal statement, description of the outcome intended, timing of the goal, and some type of accountability. For example, if one of the activities was to provide tutoring in Math for middle school students, then a S.M.A.R.T. goal might look like this:

Goal	Objective	Timeframe	Person(s) Responsible
Goal #1: To provide Math tutorial services in the after-school program for 100 middle school students	*Objective #1*: High School Student Tutor and Tutor Coach job postings	Jun-Jul	Principal and Human Resource Director for posting
	Objective #2: Tutorial Coach will be assigned to the tutors to ensure accurate tutoring techniques are provided to the middle school students	By July 15th	
	Objective #3: Tutors will be hired and trained	Within the 1st 2 weeks of the academic year	Tutorial Coach (teacher on special assignment to support after school Math) for tutorial services and tutor oversight
	Objective #4: Tutorial services will be provided 4 days per week throughout the academic year by 5 high school student tutors	Tutorial services will begin by week 3, offered M-TH from 3:15-4:45 p.m. (16 wks in Fall and 18 wks in Spring)	

TIP: The reason I recommend using the S.M.A.R.T. process is to design Goals and Objectives that can be properly analyzed in the Evaluation Plan and process once the grant is funded. Make sure what you say is something you can measure moving forward to be able to determine if you were successful or not.

Chapter 7

Sustainability Plan

The Sustainability Plan describes the foundation that the grant has laid for the organization and explains how integration into the organization for the long-term can be accomplished once the funding has come to an end. This can be one of the most challenging sections of the grant to write because long-term sustainability can require organizational change and resource allocation adjustments to maintain services after the grant comes to an end. Not all grants require this section, but if they do you must write to the prompts asked for by the funder.

In the Sustainability Plan, often organizations will want to say that they will continue to seek funding from the same or other sources to maintain the services, but this isn't what the funder necessarily wants to hear here. When this section is present in the grant, it is wanting to see how the organization will take the grant funds as a seed or pilot project and integrate it into the fabric of the organization's offerings into perpetuity. While this isn't always feasible, the plan is just that…a plan. So, speak to the ways in which the organization will use the successful results of the project to sustain key efforts moving forward; not all components must be kept and sometimes there is the need to scale back on the offering to maintain the level of services that can be afforded by the organization.

Chapter 8

Evaluation Plan

The Evaluation Plan provides the details of how the organization will determine if they have been successful in their goals and objectives, or how they will work to improve their strategies or results moving forward. This section often includes details about program and fiscal reporting as well as the organization's plan for analyzing the project activities, goals, and objectives.

In the Evaluation Plan, the organization explains a cadence of review. This is typically a weekly, bi-weekly, monthly, or quarterly review of the activities and financial spending in the grant with either the project team, fiscal team, administrators, or the governing board. It is often a good idea to connect the analysis with the Goals and Objectives section to show the fully integrated cycle of the project.For example, you could modify the above chart to now list analysis for each Goal and Objective such as:

Goal	Key Artifacts	Intervals	Intended Outcomes
Goal #1: To provide Math tutorial services in the after-school program for 100 middle school students	*Objective #1*: Tutor and Tutor Coach job announcements	Fall Semester, Quarter 3	100% Completed
	Objective #2: Roster of tutors assigned to the Tutor Coach with weekly schedule of work	Fall Semester, Quarter 3	5 Tutors Hired
	Objective #3: Sign in sheets from Tutor training	Fall Semester, Quarter 3	5 Tutors Trained
	Pre- and post-training survey of high school tutors' level of preparedness for tutorial support	Fall Semester, Quarter 3	80% Increase in Math and Tutorial strategies to use with middle school students
	Objective #4: Mid-semester, end of semester, and end-of-year middle school student surveys about tutorial services provided	Fall Semester, Quarter 4 & Spring Semester, Quarter 2	95% of Middle School Students were Satisfied or Very Satisfied with Tutorial support provided in the after-school program

When the timing of the review of activities and financial spending come up, the team(s) or individual(s) will review the activity as it relates to the plan for evaluation. For the *Program Reporting*, there would be a narrative that speaks to the level of progress or success for each Goal and its Objectives.If the Goal or Objectives were not delivered as intended, then the narrative would explain the challenges in accomplishing the activity as well as the ways in which the organization is trying to get the activity back on track or has had to pivot to a slightly different plan (if the funding monitor is ok with the shift or change in scope). For the *Fiscal Reporting*, typically there is an accounting of expenditures, encumbrances, and remaining funds. An example may look like this mid-way through the fiscal year:

CHAPTER 8

Category	Description	Proposed Amount	Jul-Sep	Oct-Dec	Jan-Mar	Apr-Jun	Remaining Amount
1000	Certificated Stipend for Tutorial Coach	$4,500	$1,250 (2.5 mos)	$1,500 (3 mos)	$0	$0	$1,750
2000	High School Student Tutors	$18,360	$2,700 (5 wks)	$5,940 (11 wks)	$0	$0	$9,720
3000	Certificated & Classified Benefits	$3,141	$632	$1,029	$0	$0	$1,480
4000	Supplies	$1,950	$500	$500	$0	$0	$950
5000	Conference Travel	$2,115	$2,115	$0	$0	$0	$0
6000	Indirect @ 5%	$1,503	$359	$448	$0	$0	$696
7000	None	$0	$0	$0	$0	$0	$0
	TOTAL	$31,569	$7,556	$9,417	$0	$0	$14,596
			100% on Target	99% on Target			

In the example above everything was on target except from October through December there was a $50 savings in supplies. This can be made up in future purchases in the second half of the year or with an end-of-the year celebration, but if that was a tutor that quit and the cost savings were higher than the $50, this would be the point at which the organization needs to monitor and track expenditures more closely in order to full spend down all of the funds. On the flip side if all the funding for supplies was at $1,500 by mid-way through the year instead of the intended $1,050 then this too should be an indicator to that the program either needs to reduce expenses or look for alternatives moving forward to complete the needs of the program successfully. The program could ask for donations from families with students in the tutoring program, solicit contributions for businesses to pay for more supplies, conduct a fundraiser to raise funds, or ask for additional support from the middle school to augment the supply needs. While the organization does not present the 100% or 99% depicted above to the funding source typically, this is used for internal purposes to monitor progress and determine if mid-year adjustments or changes are necessary.

TIP: Typically, when presenting fiscal reports, all figures are provided in whole numbers with no rounding up. These amounts should represent actual dollars spent, and if you round up the organization hasn't fully spent some of those cents that make a difference from one reporting period to the next. In the final report the organization will true up your figure to the full amount. Also, if a funder gives you the $31,569 for this Goal, it is critical that you spend the full amount. If your grant proposal projections were a little high, for example the middle school pays their tutors at $17.50/hour instead of $18/hour then you would have some cost savings in both salaries and benefits for the tutors that then you could then use the savings in another manner (as long as the agreement allows for you to make changes across category areas, and if not clear with the funding monitor). If your grant proposal projections were too low, for then you have to adjust the budget to not overspend, for example maybe you would only have the tutors work 16 weeks in the Spring instead of the intended 18 weeks. Bottom line is you want to be right at the amount provided by the funds, and when I say right at, you want to be at less than $1 difference whenever possible to demonstrate to the funding source that you were accurate in budget projections (even if a few things fluctuate through the grant period) and that the organization has the ability to execute the fiscal responsibilities of the grant. If there is a slight surplus toward the end of the grant period, purchase extra supplies that can continue to assist students or potentially have the organization do an expense transfer from their general funds that also supported the efforts of the grant, for example snacks provided at the after-school program's tutoring sessions that wasn't paid for by the grant.

Lastly, there is often a *Final Report* for the grant that often includes both quantitative and qualitative data and analysis as well as full reconciliation of the budget. The Quantitative data would be the numbers, percentages, or ratings of the Goals and Objectives throughout the grant. These will often come from # of meetings, sign in sheets, survey results,

CHAPTER 8

etc. The Qualitative data are the stories, testimonies, or experiences from the people involved in the project. This can be from informal successes shared between tutors and students, student voice solicited in narratives prompts on the surveys regarding how the program has assisted them with the Math, parent comments to the Tutor Coach or Tutors, or Math teacher comparisons of student in and out of the after-school tutorial program and homework assignment completions or test results. To have both quantitative and qualitative data to analyze, it is important that the organization is collecting and storing key artifacts throughout the year.Also, pictures or videos are always great to share if possible with the funding source such as activities in action, celebrations, or just a student showing the A+ on their latest Math test (these will not always be allowable for sharing in the final report, but can be great tools for marketing or pitching the continuation of the program with the same funding source, other funding sources, or the middle school to institutionalize the program).

Chapter 9

Budget and Budget Narrative

The Budget and Budget Narrative links the funding requested to the activities, goals, and objectives to accomplish the project. Typically, there is a range or specific amount of funds listed in the Request for Proposal (RFP) that is available to apply for. The organization will want to then create a budget that fits within the funds available, that supports the necessary personnel to accomplish the activities listed in the Project Narrative as well as any supplies, equipment, travel, etc. that is needed to ensure the project is successful. Depending on the funding available, you may have to scale the project goals and objectives up or down to fall within the allocation potential available.

Budget:

In the Budget section, this is typically a listing of the primary classification codes and a brief description of the details within each classification. Typical classification codes include:

CHAPTER 9

- 1000 Certificated or Academic Salaries
- 2000 Classified Salaries
- 3000 Employee Benefits
- 4000 Supplies & Materials
- 5000 Other Expenses
- 6000 Capital Outlay
- 7000 Other Outgoing

As an example of the Budget portion of this section, and continuing on from the after-school Math tutorial the following might be what is seen in this section:

Category	Description	Amount
1000	Certificated Stipend for Tutorial Coach @ $500/month x 9 months (7/15-12/15 and 1/15-5/15) = $4,500	$4,500
2000	High School Student Tutors @ $18/hour x 1.5 hours/day x 4 days/week x 34 weeks (16 weeks in Fall and 18 weeks in Spring) x 5 tutors = $18,360	$18,360
3000	Certificated Benefits @ 29% = $1,305 Classified Benefits @ 10% = $1,836	$3,141
4000	Supplies (Flipchart Paper, Markers, Binders) for Tutorial Training @ $250 Supplies (Pencils, Erasers, Highlighters, Paper) for Weekly Tutoring Services @ $50/week x 34 weeks = $1,700	$1,950
5000	Conference Travel: Registration Fee @ $250, Flight @ $895, Lodging @ $225/night x 3 nights, Rental Car @ $175, Per Diem for Meals @ $30/day x 4 days) = $2,115	$2,115
6000	Indirect @ 5%	$1,503
7000	None	$0
	TOTAL	$31,569

TIP: On the Salaries and Benefits, please refer to the organization's salary schedule or payment structure as well as benefit percentages for retirement, FICA, Medicare, SUI, Workers Compensation, etc. when applying the percentages as well as Per Diem rates for accuracy in the budget (above is for example purposes only).

In this example, if the grant funding accommodated this budget, then we are good to go! If the funding available was $100,000 we might add more activities or enhance the tutorial services with some incentive fieldtrips to a college or university, provide backpacks or a graphing calculator to after school Math students, supply Math study guides, add more tutors or hours or weeks of tutorial service, or additional services such as a Saturday Academy for students extremely deficient in their Math skills or who are first generation college going and need other support services such as career exploration or financial planning in preparation for educational pathways in the secondary or post-secondary level.

TIP: If there is a range of funding available from the funder, I typically will write to just below the maximum amount. So, if the funds were listed as $50,000-$250,000 my grant budget would come in at maybe $249,750 as to not look too eager for the full amount, but if you can do a good project at $125,000 double down on your efforts and ask for the near full amount.

Budget Narrative:

In the Budget Narrative section, this is typically an accompanying narrative to the chart Budget. In the Budget Narrative you would explain in more detail each category area. For example, in Category 5000 Conference Travel, you might explain in the Budget Narrative that:

Travel
    The Tutorial Coach will attend a 4-day conference during the Summer to prepare
    for the oversight and supervision of the high school student tutors in an after-
    school program as well as receive training in the latest pedagogical strategies for

CHAPTER 9

supporting Math instruction at the middle school level.

The Budget Narrative is typically 1-2 pages of support narrative to the Budget, providing the funder with a little more detail on the Budget. It should also directly tie back to the Project Narrative's activities as well as the Objective and Goals section. If there are budgeted items that don't seem to connect to the work plan, then questions are raised in the mind of the funder or reader of the proposal, and the project begins to feel disjointed and therefore the organization will lose points in these sections; and no one wants that!

Chapter 10

Submission of the Application

The final step after your focus groups, preparing the outline, starting to write to the prompts, getting feedback from key stakeholders, developing your budget, reworking your budget to fit the funding source's award amount or range of funds, agonizing over the Activities, Goals, and Objectives, strategizing on what to evaluate and the expected outcomes...now you are ready to package everything for submission.

Often there will be some informational or cover sheet type forms requested from the funding source, often with a signature from the organization's authorized signatory. Make sure that person will be accessible within 2-5 days of the grant submission date, and not on an African Safari with no cell or internet access for an e-signature.

In addition to any funder forms requested, sometimes the funding source will have a Checklist explicitly stating how they would like the package to be submitted. This Checklist will often have formatting guidelines so if it says all the narrative needs to be double spaced, 12 pt font, and 1" margins, make sure you comply. If it says to email it to a specific email address and a specific subject line title, make sure you comply. If it says to use a specific platform to upload documents to or to make three original copies bound a certain way, make sure you comply. Funders don't have a sense of humor about your creative interpretation of submitting the proposal, so what they ask for is what they want to receive and by no later than the intended deadline.

TIP: If the funder has a specific form or format for the Budget, make sure that you transfer the budget from your Excel spreadsheet or Word table into their format.

The Checklist will also typically indicate what they would like first, second, third as far as order of information in the package, but if no Checklist is provided, use the following order:

1. Executive Summary
2. Introduction
3. Need Statement
4. Project Narrative
5. Goals & Objectives
6. Sustainability
7. Evaluation
8. Budget Narrative
9. Budget

This part of the process is critical. You have probably invested somewhere between 60-120 hours in gathering and preparing all the documents, narrative, and budget details and you want to see the proposal successfully submitted. Make sure you give yourself enough time prior to the deadline to not be rushing at the last minute. I often will give myself a 1-3 day buffer to make sure I don't have any signature, technology, or missing documentation issues.

TIP: If the funding source is a state or federal agency, sometimes that is a grant solicitation platform that they will use that may require getting access as an applicant. Make sure you are doing this piece WWWAAAYYYY before you are trying to submit the final proposal, you don't want to miss the deadline because of a formality such as this.

Conclusion

There you have it! All my top recommendations for what to do to start your journey in the grants arena. I really hope you have enjoyed this guide and found it useful. I truly believe this information will help you in developing your skills, and hopefully you will have the pleasure of getting that grant award and seeing your ideas come to fruition just like I did over 25 years ago!

If you found this guide helpful, I would be very appreciative if you left a favorable review for the guide on Amazon!

www.ingramcontent.com/pod-product-compliance
Lightning Source LLC
Chambersburg PA
CBHW072056230526
45479CB00010B/1095